Taming Your Boss Without Losing Your Mind: A Brave Worker's Guide to the 12 Boss Types

Marako Marcus

Published by Marako Marcus, 2024.

Copyright Page

While every precaution has been taken in the preparation of this book, the publisher assumes no responsibility for errors or omissions, or for damages resulting from the use of the information contained herein. No part of this book may be reproduced, stored in a retrieval system, or transmitted in any form or by any means, electronic, mechanical, photocopying, recording, or otherwise, without the prior written permission of the publisher, except as permitted by applicable copyright law. The information and views expressed in this book are those of the author and do not necessarily reflect the views of any organization or entity. All names, characters, and incidents in this book are fictitious. Any resemblance to real persons, living or dead, is purely coincidental.

Taming Your Boss Without Losing Your Mind: A Brave Worker's Guide to the 12 Boss Types

First Edition, December 18, 2024.

Copyright © 2024 Marako Marcus.

Written by Marako Marcus.

Introduction: The Office Jungle – Surviving the Wild Bosses

The office. That bustling ecosystem of fluorescent lighting, endless meetings, and the ever-present hum of emails pinging away. You've been there: stuck in the middle of a conversation about quarterly reports, with a boss whose eyes have glazed over as soon as someone mentioned "KPIs." It's a daily circus, and the performers? They're all your bosses. Over my 25 years as a management consultant, coach, and facilitator, I've witnessed every type of office drama you can imagine. From explosive confrontations to the quiet, passive-aggressive sabotage, bosses come in all shapes and sizes – each with their own brand of madness.

You see, being a boss isn't easy. They're expected to motivate the team, maintain control of the ship, hit targets, and somehow stay sane in the process. But the reality is, the struggle is real. Most bosses have no idea how to manage their own people, let alone their own egos. That's where this book comes in. You see, while you can't exactly change your boss (unless you're a wizard, in which case, please stop reading this and teach me your ways), you *can* learn to manage them.

This guide is your survival manual for navigating the office jungle and dealing with the 12 most common types of bosses you'll encounter. By the end of this book, you'll understand their quirks, their strengths, and their weaknesses, and more importantly, you'll know how to handle them without pulling out your hair (or, heaven forbid, quitting your job). Trust me, I've been there.

Now, let's take a look at these 12 breeds of boss, who you'll either be nodding in recognition at or squirming uncomfortably in your seat, wondering if someone told me about your boss.

1. **The Control Freak**: This one's got their fingers in every pie, obsessing over the smallest detail. A control freak never met a micro-management opportunity they didn't like.
2. **The Ghost Boss**: Just when you need them most, *poof* – they vanish. But when the project goes south, suddenly they're materializing with a million questions.
3. **The Cheerleader**: Too much optimism, too little reality. They'll give you a pep talk before every meeting, but when it comes to actually rolling up their sleeves, they've disappeared like Houdini.
4. **The Volcano**: When they erupt, you'll be cleaning up the ashes for days. Be prepared for an unpredictable explosion of emotion, usually at the most inconvenient times.
5. **The Visionary**: Big dreams, grand ideas, but when it comes to the nitty-gritty execution? Let's just say they're not always grounded in the real world.
6. **The Spreadsheet Overlord**: If it doesn't involve numbers, charts, or graphs, it's not worth their time. Expect data overload at every turn.
7. **The Social Butterfly**: More interested in office gossip and networking than actually managing the team. At least their social calendar is full.
8. **The Rulebook**: They're the enforcer, the one who insists on policies and procedures, no exceptions. Flexibility? What's that?
9. **The Idea Tornado**: A whirlwind of ideas, suggestions, and "revolutionary" concepts. Great for brainstorming, terrible for actually getting anything done.

10. **The Zen Master**: Calm, collected, detached. A little too detached, actually. Sometimes it feels like they're in a perpetual state of meditation – but where's the leadership?
11. **The Insomniac**: The one who never sleeps, and somehow expects you to work around the clock with them. Get ready for a 2 a.m. email that's *so* important.
12. **The Diva**: Drama, attention-seeking, and a flair for the theatrical. They're like the office's personal reality show.

By understanding these 12 types, you can learn to manage your boss, and maybe even manage to keep your sanity intact. So, buckle up – the office ride is about to get a whole lot more entertaining.

Chapter 1: The Control Freak – The Boss Who Just Can't Let Go

If you've ever worked for someone who believes no one can do their job better than them, you've met the Control Freak. This boss is the one who will check your work, then check it again, then ask you to check it just one more time. They're the kind of boss who thinks "delegating" is a four-letter word and trust is something for naïve people. They hover, they micromanage, and their idea of leadership is making sure everything goes according to their plan, every single time. In fact, if you see them lurking near your desk, it's probably not because they need something—they're just double-checking that you're still working, or that the world hasn't fallen apart in their absence.

Spotting a Control Freak is pretty straightforward. They'll be the ones who ask for daily updates on the tiniest tasks, as if the office is a battlefield and every email you send is a potential landmine. They often have a very specific way they want things done and expect you to follow their exact instructions. They'll say things like, "I don't mind if you do it, but I'll have to check it," or "Just send it to me first, and I'll review." This type of boss rarely takes a step back to let things unfold organically because their comfort zone is in the trenches of every detail. They'll appear to be very hands-on, which sounds positive in theory, but in reality, it can feel suffocating.

Now, what are the strengths of a Control Freak? Well, they're meticulous, detail-oriented, and extremely reliable when it comes to ensuring things are done correctly—*their* way, of course. If you need something perfect, they'll be the ones to get it done with precision. They're also usually very organized and like things to run smoothly. When it comes to checking the fine print or catching the mistakes others miss, they're invaluable. So, if you've got a massive project full of potential errors, the Control Freak will spot them before anyone else.

But of course, the shortcomings are where it gets fun. The first one is their inability to trust anyone else to get things right. This results in burnout for both them and their team. When everything is checked, rechecked, and then checked again, creativity gets stifled. Innovation is rarely welcome because they want things done in a very specific way, and there's no room for deviation. If you have a good idea or a better method, you'll find it's often shot down before it even gets off the ground. A Control Freak doesn't just micromanage; they suffocate progress. And let's not forget the stress—because if you're constantly under the watchful eye of someone who's second-guessing everything you do, even the simplest task becomes a psychological marathon.

So, how do you manage a Control Freak without losing your mind? First off, if you're going to work with this type, you need to get comfortable with constant feedback, and I mean constant. They want to know what you're doing every step of the way, so it's on you to pre-emptively offer them updates. The trick is to give them enough information to satisfy their need for control without overwhelming them. This means being thorough, but not excessively detailed. Set up regular check-ins and provide the information they want before they have to ask. This proactive communication will help ease their anxiety, but it won't completely solve the issue.

Next, work on building trust slowly. It won't happen overnight. They'll be suspicious at first, but if you consistently deliver high-quality work without mistakes, they might just start to let go—albeit in small doses. Don't take it personally when they second-guess your work. It's not about you; it's their own issue with control. Show them that you're capable and reliable, and that will gradually reduce the need for them to hover. If you're ever in doubt, ask for clarity upfront. A Control Freak loves precision, so the more you can show that you understand exactly what they want, the easier it will be to keep them off your back.

Here's the real kicker, though: Learn to manage their expectations. A Control Freak doesn't like surprises, so keep them informed about any potential issues early. If something is off-track or could go wrong, don't wait until they notice. Bring it to them immediately and propose a solution. This will demonstrate that you're on top of things and can handle the project with minimal interference. Plus, it gives them a sense of control, which is what they crave.

Lastly, learn to keep your sanity. Working for a Control Freak is exhausting, but if you don't create boundaries, you'll burn out. Find ways to disconnect after hours, even if it means ignoring a few emails. If you keep bending to their demands, they'll never stop demanding. So, while you're delivering your work, don't forget to manage your own mental well-being. Prioritize your health, your personal life, and your peace of mind. The Control Freak can't control everything, and if they try, well, that's their problem, not yours.

Chapter 2: The Ghost Boss – The Vanishing Act

The Ghost Boss is the Houdini of the office world. One minute they're there, commanding the room, and the next, *poof*, they've vanished, leaving you to wonder if they were ever really there in the first place. If you've ever found yourself staring at an empty office or an unanswered email, only to realize your boss has been MIA for days, you've encountered the Ghost. These bosses tend to disappear just when you need them most, whether it's during a crisis, a tight deadline, or when you need some direction. It's as if they've mastered the art of being present enough to delegate, but not enough to actually help or guide.

Spotting a Ghost Boss isn't hard, but tracking their movements is. They're the ones who somehow manage to be "in meetings" or "out of town" when you need approval or input. If you're lucky, they'll reply to your emails with a one-line response or a vague "let's discuss later" that never materializes. The rest of the time, they're conveniently absent. Ghost bosses don't have a physical presence that grounds the team. Instead, they rely on you to steer the ship, often leaving you in the dark, floundering while they're off "strategizing" in a meeting that never seems to end. You might see them in the hallway, but when it comes to substantive conversations about work, you'll be chasing shadows.

The Ghost Boss's strengths lie in their ability to give you space—sometimes too much of it. They'll rarely micromanage, preferring to let you get on with it. In theory, this sounds great. You're not being smothered by their presence, and you have the autonomy to make decisions. They can also be excellent at big-picture thinking, providing the kind of visionary leadership that doesn't bog down in the weeds. If you're a self-starter and don't mind working independently, a Ghost Boss can be a dream. They trust you to get things done, and they rarely interfere.

But here's the catch: without clear communication, this independence becomes a breeding ground for confusion. You're left guessing what their expectations are, and the lack of feedback means you never quite know if you're on track. Ghosts are also notorious for their lack of involvement during critical moments. When decisions need to be made, you'll find them missing in action, leaving you to navigate the storm on your own. And when you do need their input, they often deliver it too late to make a meaningful impact, or worse, they'll swoop in at the last minute and undo everything you've done because they were too busy with something else. Their absence creates an air of uncertainty, and without their guidance, you're left to fill in the blanks.

So, how do you manage a Ghost Boss without losing your mind? First, and most importantly, get comfortable with being proactive. Ghost bosses won't come looking for you, so you need to take the initiative. If you need approval or feedback, don't wait for them to come to you. Schedule regular check-ins—whether they like it or not. If they're not around for a face-to-face meeting, send detailed emails outlining what you're working on and ask specific questions. This will not only keep them in the loop but also provide a written record of your progress. Ghosts are unlikely to give you much direct feedback, so it's up to you to be clear about what you need from them.

Another tip: set clear expectations at the outset of any project. If you're unclear about their priorities or goals, ask. Don't assume they'll explain it later when they have time—because that time never seems to come. Ask for deadlines, deliverables, and their preferred methods of communication. By establishing these parameters early on, you're laying the groundwork for a better working relationship. A Ghost Boss might not provide constant feedback, but they will appreciate your ability to work independently and meet their standards without constant prompting. If you manage to get a response, take it seriously, as it will likely be sparse and to the point.

Next, learn to interpret their absence. While they're not physically present, they might still be available in their own way. Some Ghosts are more approachable by email or chat, so if they're not around for a face-to-face, try to catch them in writing. If they're truly "ghosting" you in all forms of communication, it might be time to seek out other stakeholders who can provide the direction you need. This doesn't mean you should completely abandon them, but you should know when to pivot and get the answers from someone else. If you can manage to keep the work moving without them, they might even respect you more for it—if they notice.

Finally, embrace the unpredictability. The Ghost Boss will never be the constant source of feedback and support you might want, but you can adapt. Become the master of managing your own work. Take ownership of your responsibilities, and learn to make decisions confidently, even if you don't have their approval. In the long run, this autonomy can be empowering, but it requires a level of self-discipline and initiative. And when the Ghost does return from whatever realm they've been haunting, make sure you've made enough progress to show them that their absence didn't derail the project. After all, it's not about waiting for the Ghost to reappear; it's about making sure the work gets done, with or without their presence.

Chapter 3: The Cheerleader – The Boss Who Thinks Everything is Amazing

The Cheerleader is the type of boss who's always wearing a grin that's so wide it could fit a football team through it. They're the ones who will tell you that your report is "amazing" even when it's clearly a hot mess of half-finished thoughts and mismatched data. This boss thrives on positivity and will encourage you to "give it your best shot" even when you haven't a clue what the shot actually is. The Cheerleader doesn't have time for negativity, conflict, or any sort of criticism. In their world, everything is sunshine, rainbows, and team spirit. If they had pom-poms, they'd probably wave them in meetings. They want everyone to feel good about themselves, regardless of whether or not they've actually earned that feel-good moment.

Spotting the Cheerleader is easy. They're the one in the office who never stops smiling, no matter how bad things are. You could be on the verge of a catastrophe, and the Cheerleader will be there, clapping their hands, telling you, "Don't worry! We've got this! We're a team!" They'll give you motivational quotes, send you upbeat emails at 7 a.m., and generally inject a dose of optimism into every situation. But here's the catch: their optimism can be suffocating. While they're trying to lift everyone's spirits, they often ignore real problems. When things go wrong, they deflect the issue with a "we'll work it out together!" without addressing the core problem. They live in a world of perpetual positivity, where "failure" is just "an opportunity to try harder" rather than something to learn from.

The Cheerleader's strengths are in morale-boosting and fostering a sense of camaraderie. If you're in a slump or facing an uphill battle, this boss is the one who can rally the troops and get everyone fired up. They're the first to praise your efforts, even when you haven't quite achieved the goal. They know how to make you feel like you're part of something bigger, and that's a valuable trait when motivation is flagging. The Cheerleader can be a great person to have in your corner when you're feeling uncertain or overwhelmed, as they can lift your spirits and help you see the glass as half full, even if it's actually nearly empty.

However, their shortcomings are as glaring as their optimism. The Cheerleader often overlooks the reality of the situation. When a serious issue arises, they might gloss over it with a "let's stay positive" mantra, leaving you to deal with the fallout. They might ignore your concerns or try to reassure you with vague promises rather than taking action. If you're someone who values directness and problem-solving, the Cheerleader can be more frustrating than helpful. They often create a toxic positivity environment where no one feels comfortable discussing real problems or failures. If everything is always "fine" and "going great," there's no space for constructive criticism, and that's when things start to go awry.

So, how do you manage the Cheerleader without tearing your hair out? First, you need to understand that, deep down, they mean well. Their constant enthusiasm isn't about denying reality, it's about trying to get everyone to feel empowered. But you can't allow their upbeat attitude to drown out the need for genuine feedback. The key here is to *gently* ground them in reality. If things are going wrong, you have to be the one to bring it up. Don't wait for them to notice the problem because they likely won't. Be straightforward and don't sugarcoat the issue. The Cheerleader is likely to resist at first, deflecting the problem with an optimistic phrase or two. When that happens, don't give up. Politely but firmly highlight the real issue. Say something like, "I understand we're all trying to stay positive, but this particular problem is going to set us back unless we address it directly."

Next, learn to work within their positivity without letting it cloud your judgment. When they praise you, don't dismiss it out of hand. Take the compliments in stride, but also stay focused on what needs to be done. Use their optimism to fuel your efforts, but don't mistake it for a substitute for hard work or attention to detail. If they're giving you a pat on the back for something half-baked, be gracious, but don't let it lull you into thinking the job is done. Instead, politely steer the conversation toward the next step and highlight areas that still need improvement.

Another useful tip is to gently manage their expectations. A Cheerleader often wants to see results immediately, and they'll want to celebrate everything—even if it's only a small milestone. This can be exhausting, as you may feel pressured to constantly show progress. The trick here is to find a balance. Acknowledge their positivity, but make sure that their expectations are in line with reality. If you're halfway through a project and they're already congratulating you on success, remind them that there's still more work to do and set realistic goals for the next phase.

Lastly, don't be afraid to inject some constructive criticism into your conversations. Cheerleaders are used to being surrounded by positivity, so it's up to you to bring a healthy dose of realism to the table. When you bring up concerns, present them in a way that aligns with their positive outlook. For example, "I'm really excited about the progress we've made so far, but there are a few areas where we could do better. Let's tackle those next to make sure we're on track for the big picture." This keeps the tone positive while ensuring that the issues are addressed.

Managing a Cheerleader can be draining at times, but with a bit of patience, directness, and strategic optimism, you can turn their constant cheer into a helpful boost without getting buried under their relentless enthusiasm. Just don't forget: sometimes you'll need to bring them back down to earth.

Chapter 4: The Volcano – The Boss Who Explodes Without Warning

The Volcano is the kind of boss who can go from zero to an erupting lava flow in the blink of an eye. One moment, they're calm, collected, maybe even a little friendly, and the next, they're throwing verbal fireballs in every direction, leaving destruction in their wake. It's as though their emotions are on a tightrope, and the slightest gust of wind sends them into a meltdown. You'll know when you've encountered a Volcano because you'll hear them before you see them. Whether it's an irate phone call or a raging email, the eruption usually comes with little to no warning. It's a terrifying spectacle—flames of fury, sharp words, and a very real risk of someone getting burned.

The Volcano's strength lies in their passion and commitment to the task at hand. When they're invested, they're fully engaged, and their energy is infectious. If you need someone to champion a project or get things done with intensity, the Volcano is your person. They'll dig deep, work long hours, and push the team forward with an undeniable drive. Their bursts of energy can sometimes be exhilarating, and their urgency to get things right can lead to impressive results. They're not the type to let things slide or tolerate mediocrity. The Volcano wants excellence, and they demand it with every fiber of their being. When things are going well, their intensity can be a force to be reckoned with, inspiring a team to move mountains. Unfortunately, this high-energy approach has a downside: it's volatile.

Spotting a Volcano is simple: just wait for the eruption. You can usually sense the build-up before they blow their top—small signs like a tense silence or an ever-increasing frown. But sometimes, it comes out of nowhere, and you'll suddenly find yourself ducking for cover as they unleash their fury over something minor, like a missed deadline or a typo in an email. The eruption might seem disproportionate to the issue at hand, but that's the nature of the Volcano. When they're upset, everything feels like the end of the world. They can't just be irritated—they have to be *furious*. And the worst part? You never know how long it's going to last. The eruption could subside quickly, or you might find yourself walking on eggshells for the rest of the day, waiting for the next explosion.

The Volcano's biggest shortcoming is their unpredictability. The environment they create is one of constant tension because no one knows when they'll erupt. It's emotionally draining to work under such pressure, and the fear of setting off another volcanic outburst can keep the team on edge. Their need for control and perfectionism can overshadow the actual work that needs to get done, and in the aftermath of an explosion, the team often has to spend more time repairing relationships than focusing on the tasks at hand. Not only does this create a toxic work environment, but it also leads to burnout for everyone involved. The Volcano's highs are high, but their lows are devastating.

Now, how do you manage a boss who's basically a walking time bomb? First, you need to be prepared. The Volcano doesn't like surprises, so if you see any potential for conflict, address it early. Don't wait until it's too late. Proactively communicate problems, even small ones, before they escalate into full-blown disasters. It's better to get ahead of the issue than to be caught in the aftermath of an eruption. When you do need to bring up something negative, choose your timing carefully. Don't drop a bombshell right before a big presentation or meeting. The Volcano is already operating on high alert, so adding fuel to the fire at the wrong time is asking for trouble.

When they do erupt, don't take it personally. The Volcano isn't angry at you—it's their reaction to stress, pressure, or a sense of things slipping out of control. Their rage is often a reflection of their own anxiety. The best thing you can do is remain calm. Don't get sucked into their emotional whirlwind. Stay composed, listen to their frustrations, and let them vent. But remember, don't try to talk them down in the middle of the eruption. It's like trying to negotiate with a storm—there's no reasoning with them when they're in the thick of it. Instead, wait for the eruption to die down, and then calmly approach them to discuss the issue. Let them cool off before having a rational conversation about what went wrong and how to prevent it from happening again. This isn't the time for a heated debate or pointing fingers. Focus on finding a solution that will calm the situation and move forward.

Another tip for managing the Volcano is to set clear boundaries. They might be intense, but they're not the boss of your emotional well-being. Don't let their eruptions dictate your mood or your day. If you find yourself consistently walking on eggshells, it might be time to have an honest conversation with them about the impact their behavior is having on the team. If you're in a position to do so, speak up and suggest that the Volcano find healthier ways to express their frustration. If you're not, at least protect your own mental state. Set emotional boundaries, and don't absorb their stress. Focus on the work, not the drama.

Lastly, help the Volcano learn to channel their energy more productively. When things are calm, talk to them about their triggers and how they can respond in more measured ways when things don't go according to plan. They need to understand that while passion is important, blowing up at every mistake only creates chaos. Offer them tools for managing their emotions—whether it's meditation, deep breathing, or simply taking a short walk to cool off. Encourage them to build a coping strategy for stress so that when pressure builds, they can release it without causing an earthquake in the office.

In short, dealing with a Volcano requires a steady hand, emotional intelligence, and a lot of patience. When managed properly, their intensity can become a valuable asset. But if left unchecked, their eruptions will leave a trail of destruction in their wake. The key is to keep the lava flow contained and prevent the eruption from consuming everyone around you.

Chapter 5: The Visionary – Big Ideas, No Real Plan

The Visionary is a boss who lives in the clouds and expects you to join them in their lofty ideas. They're constantly talking about the next big thing, a project that could change the company, or a concept that will revolutionize the industry. They have a mind that's full of grand visions, and they're always excited about the future. However, you'll quickly learn that their enthusiasm is often not grounded in any concrete plan. It's all big ideas and no action.

Spotting a Visionary is easy—they're the ones who constantly walk into meetings with a new concept that "could change everything," while you're sitting there wondering how the current strategy is still not implemented. You'll find them scribbling on napkins, passionately discussing what the future could look like, and often hinting at ideas that sound amazing but lack a practical path to get there. You'll know you've encountered a Visionary when their thoughts tend to jump from one big idea to the next without ever seeing anything through. They thrive on innovation but rarely bring anything to completion. They're often frustratingly vague, and you might find yourself scrambling for clarification while they move on to the next brainstorm session.

The Visionary's strength lies in their ability to inspire. They've got energy, passion, and the kind of enthusiasm that makes you feel like you're part of something transformative. If you're someone who loves thinking big and embracing change, working with a Visionary can be exciting. They make you believe that anything is possible, and they're usually the kind of leaders who'll encourage you to think outside the box and break the rules. They also tend to be excellent at spotting emerging trends or seeing opportunities that others miss, which can lead to breakthroughs when harnessed correctly.

However, their biggest shortcoming is the complete lack of follow-through. The Visionary is great at starting projects but terrible at finishing them. They'll have a plan in their head, but it often lacks the necessary details to actually get it off the ground. They're big-picture thinkers, but they can't always translate that into a workable strategy. This leaves their team in a constant state of "what now?" because the Visionary's ideas are often unrefined and incomplete. They want you to be just as excited about their latest brainstorm as they are, but without a roadmap, you're left trying to figure out how to execute something that's never really been fully planned.

So, how do you work with a Visionary without pulling your hair out in frustration? First, it's essential to help them focus. They need someone who can take their lofty ideas and turn them into actionable plans. This isn't about raining on their parade, but about being the practical voice that helps translate their big dreams into small, achievable steps. If they say, "Let's build a new app that changes the world," your job is to ask, "What's the first step in making that happen?" If they can't provide an answer, it's up to you to start mapping out the basics. Break down the large idea into smaller, manageable parts that can be tackled incrementally. The Visionary thrives on excitement, but they need structure to make things happen.

When working with a Visionary, it's crucial to be proactive. They're not likely to give you a clear set of instructions, so you'll need to take the initiative. Expect to do a lot of the heavy lifting in terms of organizing and executing the vision. You might need to draft timelines, budgets, and action plans, and present these back to them in a way that fuels their excitement without stifling it. Visionaries often get caught up in the potential of an idea but fail to see the hard work that goes into making it a reality. You're there to remind them of the practical side and keep the momentum going.

Communication is another vital area to keep in check. A Visionary will want to discuss ideas for hours, and it's your job to bring them back to earth when necessary. Don't be afraid to challenge them, but do it in a way that keeps the conversation focused. Help them articulate the steps necessary to turn their idea into something tangible. For example, ask them about the resources required, potential obstacles, and who needs to be involved. Bring in data and examples to support your points, because while the Visionary thrives on enthusiasm, you'll need concrete information to anchor them.

One of the biggest challenges in working with a Visionary is keeping them accountable. They often don't want to deal with the nitty-gritty details or the follow-up required to see their ideas come to life. If you want to make sure the vision is actualized, you'll need to be persistent. Set clear milestones and deadlines for them and the team, and regularly check in to ensure progress is being made. A Visionary can easily get distracted by the next big idea, so it's up to you to ensure the current one doesn't get lost in the shuffle.

The key to working with a Visionary is balance. Embrace their big ideas, but don't get swept away by the excitement. Bring practicality to the table, and be prepared to roll up your sleeves and take charge of turning their dreams into reality. The Visionary is an excellent source of inspiration, but without someone to help bring their visions to life, all that creativity is just a series of empty promises. So, keep them focused, organized, and on track, and you'll be able to turn their grand ideas into something you can both be proud of.

Chapter 6: The Spreadsheet Overlord – The Boss Who Lives and Breathes Data

The Spreadsheet Overlord is the boss who thinks Excel is the answer to all of life's problems. If it's not on a spreadsheet, it doesn't exist in their world. Their obsession with numbers, formulas, and data borders on the pathological. They can whip up a pivot table faster than most people can make a cup of coffee, and if you need to make a decision, the Spreadsheet Overlord will direct you straight to the most complex, soul-crushing report you've ever seen. And don't even think about making a move without consulting the spreadsheet first. The idea of gut instinct or creative thinking is foreign to them. For the Spreadsheet Overlord, data is not just a tool—it's the Bible, the Constitution, and the Ten Commandments all rolled into one.

So, how do you spot a Spreadsheet Overlord? It's not difficult—just follow the trail of numbers. They'll probably be hunched over their desk, deep in the throes of a new data analysis, their eyes bloodshot from hours of looking at rows and columns. When you approach them, the first thing they'll do is pull up some form of data to justify every single decision they've ever made. They're the kind of boss who doesn't believe in "gut feel" or "creative intuition." They need data to validate every single step. If the team is discussing a new project, expect them to present an overwhelming slide deck filled with charts, tables, and graphs that no one actually wants to look at but will pretend to understand because, well, that's what the Spreadsheet Overlord expects.

The strength of the Spreadsheet Overlord lies in their precision and their ability to make data-driven decisions. When it comes to numbers, they're second to none. They can spot trends in data with the sharpness of a hawk, and they'll never make an impulsive decision based on a hunch. This is the boss who will always back up their decisions with cold, hard evidence. Their attention to detail is unmatched, and their ability to organize vast amounts of information into digestible, understandable formats is a skill that any business can benefit from. When you need something thoroughly researched, methodically planned, and backed by facts, the Spreadsheet Overlord is your go-to. If you're trying to get a budget approved or justify a new initiative, they'll bring a well-crafted spreadsheet that not only convinces everyone in the room but also makes you feel like you're being led through a financial maze.

But the shortcomings of the Spreadsheet Overlord are equally glaring. For one, they're emotionally clueless. They can't see the forest for the trees. All the charts, formulas, and graphs in the world won't help them manage people or read the room. If the data says everything is fine, they'll refuse to acknowledge that the team might be burnt out, frustrated, or in need of a little encouragement. The Spreadsheet Overlord's world is one of facts and figures, and that's all they'll ever trust. There's no room for nuance or human judgment in their approach. This can make them incredibly difficult to work with, especially in situations that require flexibility or a creative solution. And don't even think about asking them to make a decision without data—you'll just get a cold stare and a lecture on the importance of numbers.

Managing a Spreadsheet Overlord is a delicate balance. First, if you want to get anything done, don't try to appeal to their emotions or subjective reasoning. You'll lose. Instead, come prepared with data. You'll need to arm yourself with cold, hard facts that support your case. If you're proposing a new project, make sure you've done your homework. If you're going to convince them that a new initiative is worth pursuing, show them the numbers. Use charts, graphs, or anything else that speaks their language. Data is the currency of the Spreadsheet Overlord, so the more you can provide, the better.

Next, understand that the Spreadsheet Overlord's need for data doesn't just end with decision-making—it's in every part of their life. When they ask for a status update on a project, they won't want a simple summary. They'll want a detailed report, with milestones, timelines, and progress metrics. If you don't have those, be prepared for them to make you feel like you're wasting their time. While this might seem frustrating, it's actually an opportunity for you to prove your value. If you can get ahead of the game and present well-organized, data-driven reports, you'll earn their respect. It might not feel like it's about people, but to the Spreadsheet Overlord, a well-crafted spreadsheet is a reflection of your professionalism. It shows you're detail-oriented, reliable, and capable. Get used to the idea that if you want to get things done with them, you need to speak their language—and that language is numbers.

However, don't get too comfortable in their world of Excel. As much as they love data, they can be blind to everything that isn't represented on a spreadsheet. This is where you need to step in with a little emotional intelligence. When the Spreadsheet Overlord starts spinning their web of numbers and charts, remind them gently—very gently—that there's more to the picture than just what's on the page. If the team is stressed, let them know. If there's a problem brewing that isn't immediately obvious in the numbers, point it out in a way that brings it back to their beloved spreadsheets. For example, you might say, "I've noticed a downward trend in employee engagement, and while the numbers still look fine, it might be worth investigating further." This approach will keep them from dismissing the human side of things while still catering to their need for data.

In short, working with a Spreadsheet Overlord requires patience, preparation, and a solid understanding of numbers. If you can provide the data they crave and navigate the conversations in their world, you'll be seen as a valuable asset. Just don't expect them to throw a big celebration when things go well. For the Spreadsheet Overlord, success is simply another box to tick on their checklist.

Chapter 7: The Social Butterfly – The Boss Who'd Rather Be Networking Than Working

The Social Butterfly is that boss who somehow spends more time chatting by the coffee machine than getting things done. Their day is filled with meetings, but not the productive kind. No, they're the ones who are always in the middle of the office gossip, organizing the next "team-building" event, or hosting lunch with the latest colleague they've just met. When they're not throwing parties or arranging happy hours, they're most likely popping in and out of your workspace, asking about your weekend plans, your thoughts on the latest office drama, and anything else that will make them seem like the friendly, approachable boss everyone loves. But don't expect them to actually take action on any work-related issue—they're far too busy schmoozing with the next person on their radar.

You'll spot a Social Butterfly boss by the trail of conversations they leave in their wake. They're always surrounded by people, drawing attention to themselves with their "people person" persona. They often pop up in the middle of projects to offer some unsolicited "encouragement," but they tend to do this in a way that feels more like an interruption than a boost. They rarely sit still for long and seem to always have somewhere to go, whether it's a quick chat with HR, a call with an important client, or a spontaneous lunch date with a colleague. If you ever find yourself trying to get a solid answer from them on a project detail, you're likely to get distracted with an unrelated topic—like the latest office rumors, or even their thoughts on the best new coffee blend in the break room. Bottom line: their focus is anything but focused.

The strength of the Social Butterfly boss lies in their ability to connect people. They're the glue that holds the team together, often playing the role of the office peacemaker, the motivator, and the one who boosts morale when things start to feel a little too serious. If there's a problem in the team, the Social Butterfly will have already heard about it—by the time it hits your inbox, they'll have already gathered enough intel from various sources to offer a diplomatic solution. They thrive in environments that require collaboration and networking, and they know how to make people feel comfortable and heard. If there's a big project that requires team buy-in, the Social Butterfly will be your best ally. They know how to get people on board by making them feel included and valued.

But while they're great at managing relationships, they're not so great at managing results. The Social Butterfly can be extremely good at keeping everyone happy, but they'll often neglect the critical task of keeping things on track. Deadlines are mere suggestions to them, and when things inevitably start slipping through the cracks, they tend to rely on charm and a smile to smooth things over. It's not that they don't care about the work; it's just that they care more about making sure everyone is on good terms, which can sometimes lead to a lack of focus on what's really important. The more serious, analytical tasks that require undivided attention might fall to the wayside when there's another party to plan, or when the next big chat with someone in the hallway takes priority.

Managing a Social Butterfly boss is an exercise in patience and strategy. If you want to get things done, you'll have to be assertive without coming off as rude. First, make it clear that while you value their enthusiasm for team bonding and morale, you also need to get things done. The Social Butterfly might take a few moments to process this, but they'll generally appreciate the gentle reminder that work comes before play (at least occasionally). Instead of waiting for them to direct the team, take the reins and schedule structured check-ins or provide a clear agenda. You might need to be the one to push for deadlines and ensure that everyone stays on track. While the Social Butterfly will be happy to connect with people and encourage collaboration, it's up to you to ensure the actual work gets completed.

When you need something from them, don't hesitate to be direct. They might not be the type to sit down and hash out the details of a project in a meeting, but they'll respond well if you approach them with a clear ask. Keep your requests concise, and be sure to frame them in a way that taps into their people-oriented strengths. For example, instead of saying, "I need approval on this budget," try, "Can you help me get buy-in for this budget with the team? They'll listen to you, and I could use your support." This way, you're appealing to their strength in networking and getting people on board, rather than asking them to dive into a detailed report they won't care about.

However, while it's important to recognize their networking abilities, don't let them off the hook for actual results. Be ready to hold them accountable. When the team's morale is high, you'll want to capitalize on that energy and ensure it translates into productivity. It's not enough for the Social Butterfly to just be well-liked—they need to lead the charge when it comes to execution. If they start to veer off course, pull them back in with gentle reminders that results are equally important. Present these reminders in a way that acknowledges their strengths but also underscores the importance of maintaining focus. For example, "I love that everyone's excited about the new project—let's make sure we also have some hard deadlines to keep things on track."

In the end, working with a Social Butterfly boss requires a mix of empathy, clarity, and a bit of finesse. You'll need to guide them back to the task at hand when they get distracted, but you should also take advantage of their natural ability to motivate and engage others. With the right approach, you'll be able to harness their people skills while ensuring the work gets done—without turning into a party planner yourself.

Chapter 8: The Rulebook – The Boss Who Lives and Breathes Policies

The Rulebook boss is a walking manual of company policies, procedures, and regulations. If you need to know the proper protocol for sending an email, taking a lunch break, or even making a coffee run, they've got it memorized. Their job seems to be enforcing rules—any rules—because rules, as far as they're concerned, are the foundation of all good work. They'll be the first to point out that you've missed a step in the process or haven't followed procedure to the letter. Don't even think about bending the rules. In their eyes, a rule is a rule, and bending them is a one-way ticket to failure. If the company policy states that reports must be submitted by 5 p.m., then don't even dare try to submit it at 5:05 p.m. or you'll get the "didn't we discuss this last time?" speech. They are champions of consistency, order, and fairness, but this rigid approach doesn't always win them the popularity contest.

You'll spot a Rulebook boss by their obsession with paperwork, schedules, and order. They keep a neat, tidy desk, because chaos is simply not an option. They don't just know the company's rules; they can recite them in their sleep. Their calendar is packed with back-to-back meetings, most of which are to ensure that everyone follows the exact procedures, whether that's approving a process or checking in on compliance. The Rulebook boss will often interrupt casual conversations to remind you of the right way to do something, and you'll find yourself frequently hearing phrases like "That's not how we do it here" or "Please refer to section three, paragraph B." They don't do spontaneity, creativity, or flexibility.

To them, the rules are the only way to maintain order in an otherwise chaotic world.

The strength of the Rulebook boss is their reliability. If you need consistency, they're your person. They'll never surprise you with a last-minute change or fail to follow through on a commitment—unless, of course, the commitment violates some sort of procedure. They are dependable, often keeping projects on track by sticking to deadlines, budgets, and methods. This makes them excellent at roles that require accuracy, detail, and a clear set of instructions. They ensure that everyone knows what's expected of them and make sure that nothing falls through the cracks. If you want something done by the book, the Rulebook boss is your go-to. They can be relied upon to ensure that the team is operating within the company's established framework, which, of course, is precisely how things should be done.

However, the Rulebook boss's love affair with policies and procedures often comes at the expense of flexibility and creativity. The downside is their inability to adapt. If a situation requires a bit of thinking outside the box or a shift in approach, the Rulebook boss is likely to freeze up. Their focus on processes often blinds them to the nuances of a situation. This can be especially frustrating when the team is trying to navigate an issue that doesn't have a clear solution in the rulebook. The Rulebook boss's lack of flexibility can lead to inefficiency, frustration, and sometimes stagnation, as they become bogged down in the details instead of finding a practical solution. Creativity? They see it as a deviation from the plan.

So, how do you manage a Rulebook boss without losing your will to live? First, you have to recognize that while they may be stuck in their ways, their commitment to the rules is not malicious—it's just who they are. Start by being clear, precise, and organized when you present your work to them. They don't want to hear your creative flair or innovative ideas unless it's wrapped in a nice, tidy proposal with all the correct citations, steps, and references. It's not that they don't want innovation; it's just that they prefer it within the confines of a structured framework. If you want to suggest a new approach or a change to a process, be prepared to show them how it fits within existing guidelines. Frame your suggestions within the language they understand: "Here's a potential solution that still adheres to our policy, but it might improve efficiency."

In meetings, keep your discussions on track and avoid getting sidetracked by big-picture ideas or abstract concepts. The Rulebook boss isn't interested in philosophical debates or hypothetical situations. Stick to facts, numbers, and data. If the conversation starts veering into the realm of creativity or brainstorming, gently steer it back to practicality. You can also manage expectations by reminding them of the importance of flexibility in certain situations, but be prepared for them to bristle. The Rulebook boss values stability and predictability, and any suggestion to deviate from the rules will likely meet resistance. Your best bet is to show them the practical benefits of change through hard evidence and examples.

If you're the one leading a project under a Rulebook boss, be ready to provide regular updates and document everything. They'll want to see progress reports, risk assessments, and everything else you can throw their way. Do not skip steps. If something goes wrong, don't try to cover it up—be transparent. They respect honesty and adherence to protocols, even if that means admitting a mistake. But don't be surprised if they remind you how the mistake could have been avoided by following the rules more closely. The Rulebook boss is big on accountability, and they'll expect you to hold yourself and others to the same standards.

The key to working with a Rulebook boss is to meet their need for structure and consistency while gently nudging them toward a bit more flexibility when necessary. Be organized, be direct, and always respect the rules—unless, of course, you can convince them that breaking a rule might actually be the more efficient solution. And even then, make sure you've got a solid, step-by-step explanation ready for why it's in everyone's best interest. They may not be fans of change, but if you present it correctly, you might just make them see the light—while sticking firmly to the rulebook, of course.

Chapter 9: The Idea Tornado – The Boss Who Can't Stop Spinning Ideas

The Idea Tornado is the boss who walks into the office every morning with a new concept, a fresh idea, and a vision so grand it could make your head spin. If you've ever felt like you've been swept up in a whirlwind of possibilities with no clear direction, congratulations, you've encountered the Idea Tornado. This boss is full of enthusiasm and innovation—at least on the surface. They live for brainstorming sessions and thrive on the excitement of a new idea. Problem is, they rarely see any of those ideas through to completion. It's all about the thrill of the next big thing, and the last one? Well, that's already been abandoned for something more exciting. If there's a "shiny object" in the room, you can bet the Idea Tornado is distracted by it and wants to chase it.

You'll spot the Idea Tornado by the constant stream of new projects and plans they present. One moment, they're talking about transforming the company culture, and the next, they're planning to introduce a whole new product line. Their calendar is packed with meetings that often end in more ideas being thrown around than actual decisions being made. They love the creative process—the chaos, the excitement, and the energy. However, when it comes to turning these ideas into reality, well, they're not exactly the best at following through. You might hear them say things like "We'll circle back to this!" or "Let's put a pin in it!" But the truth is, they rarely circle back, and that pin remains firmly in place. If you've ever wondered whether you'll ever see that project through, you probably won't.

The strength of the Idea Tornado lies in their boundless creativity and ability to inspire those around them. They're the ones who'll get you thinking in new ways, seeing opportunities where you once saw obstacles. If you need a fresh perspective or a way to shake things up, they're your person. They push the boundaries and encourage innovation, which is great when you're stuck in a rut. Their energy can be infectious, and they can get a whole team excited about new initiatives, making them fantastic at setting the stage for creative breakthroughs. If you're looking for someone who'll encourage you to step outside your comfort zone, the Idea Tornado is your cheerleader.

However, their shortcomings are impossible to ignore. The Idea Tornado is often more focused on the big picture than on the details, and this is where they fall short. They love the beginning of a project, the spark of an idea, but they struggle to manage the follow-through. It's like watching a race car rev its engine at the starting line, only for it to sit there idling forever. They want to be ahead of the curve and jump into the next thing without addressing what's already on the table. This means that many of their brilliant ideas end up shelved, forgotten, or worse, half-finished with no clear direction. The problem isn't the creativity—it's the execution. They can easily overwhelm the team with too many projects, all of which require attention but none of which get completed. And while the Idea Tornado's enthusiasm is often contagious, it can also be exhausting if you're stuck trying to keep up with their endless ideas without any solid plans to show for it.

So how do you manage an Idea Tornado boss without losing your mind? First, understand that their heart is in the right place—they're not throwing new ideas at you just to create chaos. They genuinely believe that their ideas will make a difference, and they want you to be excited too. The trick is to set boundaries. The next time they throw a shiny new idea your way, don't just nod and smile. Instead, take a step back and ask practical questions: "What's the timeline for this?" "How does this fit with our current goals?" "What resources do we need?" A bit of grounding will help steer the conversation away from pure fantasy and into something more actionable. While the Idea Tornado might not want to get bogged down by details, it's your job to rein them in. Ask them to prioritize the ideas and focus on the most promising ones. Sometimes, all it takes is a gentle reminder that they can't tackle everything at once.

Another way to work with the Idea Tornado is by giving them the space to brainstorm, but then quickly move into execution mode. If you're part of a team, don't let the ideas stagnate. As soon as the idea is out there, agree on the next steps immediately. Set clear goals, deadlines, and assign responsibilities. The Idea Tornado will likely be happy to hand off the details to someone else, so make sure the execution is in capable hands. Follow up regularly, keep the momentum going, and remind them of the progress made. This way, they're not left wandering aimlessly, and you're not stuck chasing after every idea that comes out of their mouth.

If you find yourself in a leadership role under an Idea Tornado boss, you have to be the steady hand on the wheel. You need to take their enthusiasm and turn it into something tangible. Gently challenge them to commit to an idea and stay the course. It's a delicate dance—be supportive of their creativity but help them focus. Set clear expectations and hold them accountable to follow through. Sometimes you may need to step in and make the tough decision to pull the plug on an idea if it's not working. The Idea Tornado won't love that, but they'll respect you for keeping things from spiraling into a whirlwind of chaos.

Ultimately, managing the Idea Tornado is about creating structure around their creativity. Let them dream, let them inspire, but don't let them drown the team in unfinished projects. You might never stop the tornado from spinning, but with a little direction, you can at least keep the debris to a minimum.

Chapter 10: The Zen Master – The Boss Who's Too Calm for Their Own Good

The Zen Master is the boss who is perpetually calm, collected, and seemingly at peace with everything—no matter how chaotic things get. They walk into the office with a sense of inner serenity that you could only dream of achieving in your most peaceful moments of meditation. They are the picture of calm in the storm, which, let's face it, can be both reassuring and irritating. You'll spot them when everyone else is running around, frantic and overwhelmed, and your boss is sitting at their desk with a cup of tea, completely unruffled, as if the world isn't crumbling around them. If you've ever wondered if your boss is secretly a monk, you've probably met a Zen Master.

The thing is, their calmness can be contagious—if you're the type who thrives on peace and quiet. But for the rest of us, it can feel like they're missing in action. Their unflappable nature means they don't seem to get stressed about anything, even when it's obvious that they should. When everyone else is scrambling to meet deadlines, your Zen Master is in the corner, calmly sipping their tea and giving off the vibe of someone who's on holiday in a tropical paradise. They're the type who'll tell you everything is fine when the office is on fire, and yes, the metaphorical fire could be burning down your projects, your client relationships, and possibly your career, but they'll just reassure you with an "It'll work itself out."

What's often frustrating about the Zen Master is that they don't seem to feel urgency, and they certainly don't communicate it well to others. If something is important, they'll quietly acknowledge it and then let it simmer on the back burner. For them, there's no need to rush or get stressed; everything has a way of unfolding in its own time. While that might sound like a perfectly acceptable way of navigating life in a yoga class, in the high-speed world of business, it can come across as detached, aloof, and disengaged. Deadlines? Pfft. They believe in the "universe will align" approach. Projects that need attention? They'll get around to them—eventually.

What the Zen Master excels at is maintaining stability. In a crisis, they're the ones you want in charge, as they won't buckle under pressure. They won't panic or make rash decisions. The Zen Master will think through the situation with calm deliberation and often present a rational, level-headed response when everyone else is on the brink of a nervous breakdown. Their strength is in maintaining the big picture perspective, which is great when your team is caught up in the whirlwind of minor details. They provide a steady hand, and they can help everyone else keep their cool.

But here's the problem: when a sense of urgency is required, the Zen Master can be completely ineffective. While they can bring calm to chaos, they might miss the urgency needed in situations that require quick, decisive action. If your project is behind schedule and everyone is scrambling to catch up, you don't need someone sitting there humming quietly, meditating on the situation. You need someone who can light a fire under the team and get them moving. The Zen Master's lack of urgency can lead to missed deadlines, lack of momentum, and a general feeling that things are slipping through the cracks. While they may see themselves as a calming presence, others may perceive them as lazy, disengaged, or indifferent. And that's when you start to get annoyed because while you're running around doing the heavy lifting, they're sipping tea and listening to calming music.

Now, let's talk about how to manage or work better with the Zen Master. First of all, understand that their calmness comes from a place of confidence—it's not apathy. They believe in the power of letting things unfold, and they don't feel the need to micromanage or control every situation. They trust the process and the people involved, which is a rare quality in today's work environment. But you'll need to work with that. You need to create a balance between their zen-like patience and the action-oriented demands of the workplace. When you approach them with an issue, don't just say, "We're behind schedule." That's too vague for the Zen Master, and you'll get a shrug. Instead, lay out the problem in terms of action: "This is what's at risk. Here's the immediate next step we need to take to fix it." Paint a clear picture of what needs to happen, and emphasize the urgency. The Zen Master will appreciate the clarity, and you might just get them to snap out of their peaceful reverie and spring into action.

If you find yourself under a Zen Master boss, the key is to be proactive. They won't chase you down for progress updates or deadlines. It's up to you to keep them informed and make sure things don't slide. Keep them on track by scheduling regular check-ins, where you can report on the status of various tasks and gently remind them of any upcoming deadlines. You'll need to take on the role of the driver, while they take a step back and offer guidance from the passenger seat. But don't be surprised if, in the middle of your detailed report, they interrupt with a story about how a meditation retreat changed their life. It's just part of their charm—or lack thereof.

If you're a leader working under a Zen Master, consider introducing a bit more structure to their world. They thrive when they can have space to think, but that doesn't mean they should be left alone in a room full of half-completed projects. You'll need to gently encourage them to commit to deadlines and set clearer priorities. Sometimes, the best way to help them lead effectively is to provide them with a framework that forces them to make quicker decisions. They might resist at first, but with a little patience and guidance, they'll realize that their calm demeanor can coexist with getting things done—at least some of the time.

Ultimately, working with a Zen Master is all about balance. You can benefit from their calm energy, but you'll need to ensure that their tranquility doesn't turn into a roadblock. Keep them focused, stay proactive, and you'll be able to turn their peaceful approach into a powerful tool for steady progress. Just don't expect them to ever get flustered—they've mastered the art of not caring about deadlines.

Chapter 11: The Insomniac – The Boss Who Never Sleeps and Expect You to Keep Up

The Insomniac is the boss who's always awake and working, no matter the time of day—or night. They're the one who sends you an email at 3 a.m., then expects a reply before your coffee break. You know who they are when your phone pings at odd hours, and it's their name lighting up your screen with a new task or an unsolicited bit of feedback. They're the ones who don't believe in weekends, or taking a day off. For them, it's a badge of honor to be constantly 'on,' responding to emails at all hours, working through lunch, and sprinting from one project to the next without even stopping to catch their breath. They act like sleep is for the weak, and they think their endless work ethic is something to be admired.

How do you spot them? Easy. The Insomniac is the one who sends you messages at absurd hours, always has a new project in mind, and asks you to meet right before your evening plans. Their calendar is packed, their emails flood in nonstop, and they believe productivity comes from sheer exhaustion rather than balance. They'll brag about how little sleep they get and how they "just don't need it." You might hear them mention how they "grind" all day, every day, like it's a sign of their exceptional dedication. And if you try to bring up the idea of rest or work-life balance, they'll probably dismiss it as something for "less committed" employees.

The Insomniac might be pushing themselves to the limit, but they're likely pushing you right along with them. They tend to think that the more hours you work, the better your results. But there's a flaw in their logic: productivity isn't a direct equation of hours worked. Eventually, constant work without rest leads to burnout, lack of focus, and mistakes. But try telling that to the Insomniac. They'll brush off your concerns as "excuses," convinced that the only way to succeed is by being on the clock 24/7.

What the Insomniac excels at is sheer determination. They're incredibly driven, and they can work tirelessly to meet deadlines. They push through obstacles and have an uncanny ability to keep going long after others would have thrown in the towel. When the pressure's on, the Insomniac thrives, often staying up late to finish projects or come up with new ideas. They are excellent at getting results, even if it means sacrificing personal well-being. Their dedication can be contagious, inspiring the team to push through long hours to meet goals. They'll lead by example, often setting the pace for everyone else, and for some people, that might be motivating.

But there's a massive downside: the Insomniac's relentless focus on work can lead to serious burnout. They're not great at recognizing their own limits, let alone the limits of their team. Their idea of productivity is quantity over quality. The lack of breaks and down time isn't sustainable, and the Insomniac's constant pace can make the work environment feel more like a pressure cooker than a place to innovate. Their approach can breed resentment in teams who feel overworked, underappreciated, and constantly on edge. They don't respect the need for personal time, and they'll often push people to stay late, ignore holidays, and cancel vacations. It's their version of "commitment," but it's hardly a healthy work culture.

Working with the Insomniac requires a strategic approach. First, you need to acknowledge their work ethic. Don't dismiss it outright, because they do get results—but you'll need to make sure you don't fall into the trap of working yourself to exhaustion. If you're on their team, the first thing you should do is manage your own boundaries. The Insomniac will keep pushing for more, and if you let them, you'll burn out faster than a faulty lightbulb. Be firm about your limits, and stick to them. Set clear expectations about when you'll be available and when you won't. If they insist on contacting you at ridiculous hours, politely remind them that your workday ends at a reasonable time. They might grumble, but they'll respect you for drawing a line.

Second, you'll need to be proactive in managing your workload. The Insomniac won't always have the best sense of when to delegate, so it's up to you to ensure tasks are being distributed effectively. Don't wait for them to micromanage; take the initiative to ask for clarification on priorities and deadlines. They might bombard you with requests, but if you stay organized and keep communication clear, you'll be able to maintain some semblance of control. Keep them updated on progress regularly, so they can't accuse you of slacking off. At the same time, be smart about the tasks you take on—don't fall into the trap of accepting everything that comes your way. Prioritize what matters and politely turn down the things that will stretch you too thin.

Lastly, recognize that the Insomniac's idea of leadership is often to lead by example, but that doesn't mean you have to follow in their footsteps. While they may expect you to mirror their tireless work ethic, don't let them drag you into unhealthy habits. Focus on your own well-being, and make sure you're taking breaks, setting boundaries, and doing the work that matters. If the Insomniac pushes for more hours or demands more energy than you can give, gently remind them of the need for quality work over constant output. Explain that taking breaks and pacing yourself actually leads to better results in the long term. It may take some time to get through to them, but ultimately, you can help them see that working smarter, not harder, is the key to success.

In the end, managing the Insomniac is about managing your own time and boundaries. While they might be a source of constant stress, with the right approach, you can survive their demanding work style without losing your sanity. Keep the work quality high, set clear limits, and remind the Insomniac that while they may never need sleep, the rest of us still do.

Chapter 12: The Diva – The Boss Who Thinks the World Revolves Around Them

The Diva is that boss who believes the entire office exists to serve their every whim. They thrive on attention, and they can turn even the most mundane situation into a full-blown spectacle. They want the spotlight at all times, and they'll make sure you know when they're not getting it. Whether it's the dramatic sigh when their coffee isn't made exactly to their liking or a full-blown performance when things don't go according to plan, they'll make sure the room knows who's in charge—and it's them. If you've ever worked with someone who insists on turning the smallest mistake into a crisis or demands constant affirmation for the most trivial accomplishments, you've met the Diva.

How do you spot them? Simple. They are always the center of attention, and if they aren't, they'll make sure they are. If a problem arises, they'll make it known that the entire world is falling apart around them, and they will not hesitate to let you know how their day is ruined. They throw tantrums when things don't go their way, which can range from passive-aggressive comments to full-on dramatic outbursts. The Diva is the boss who demands praise like it's oxygen, expects everything to be done their way, and has no issue making things uncomfortable to make their point. You can usually spot them by the way they dress (always stylish, always making a statement), their tendency to be overly involved in the office gossip, and their knack for creating drama in even the most mundane situations.

Their strengths? Well, they're not entirely useless, despite their flair for the theatrical. The Diva knows how to command attention, and when they're on their game, they can inspire a team with their passion and energy. They often have a sharp sense of what works and what doesn't, and when they're in a good mood, they can be an excellent motivator, driving people to push harder and perform better. They excel in high-pressure environments where a bit of flair and drama might actually keep the team engaged. They can make even the most boring task feel like a victory with just the right amount of hype. When they get their way, they can be a powerful force, leading projects to completion with enthusiasm, energy, and an unwavering belief in their vision.

However, the shortcomings are where the fun really begins. The Diva's need for attention and constant validation can create a toxic atmosphere in the workplace. They struggle with criticism, especially when it's delivered constructively. They're prone to taking offense at the smallest remarks and may make passive-aggressive comments or create a scene when things don't go as planned. If something doesn't go according to their grand vision, you'll know about it. Instead of fixing the issue, the Diva would rather make sure everyone knows that it's someone else's fault, often throwing team members under the proverbial bus to save face. Their emotional outbursts can make others feel like they're walking on eggshells, constantly trying to avoid triggering the next dramatic moment. They tend to take credit for successes but shy away from any responsibility when things go wrong. In the worst cases, they create an environment of fear and anxiety, where everyone is just waiting for the next "performance" to unfold.

Now, managing the Diva is an art form in itself. First and foremost, you need to stay calm. No matter how dramatic their outbursts are, you cannot react in kind. If you do, you'll find yourself in a never-ending cycle of theatrics that never ends well. Instead, stay grounded, be professional, and don't feed into the drama. When they demand attention or praise, give it to them in a way that feels genuine but doesn't leave you feeling like a mere pawn in their emotional game. Acknowledge their contributions without going overboard, because once you start inflating their ego, it's like feeding a black hole.

When the Diva starts to throw a tantrum, your best bet is to calmly address the situation, but don't get sucked into the emotional whirlpool. Stick to the facts and avoid getting personal. If they're upset about something that went wrong, acknowledge their feelings, but also remind them of the bigger picture. Gently steer the conversation toward solutions rather than dwelling on the problem. If they start blaming everyone else, step in and redirect the conversation toward finding a way forward instead of continuing the blame game.

Dealing with their need for constant validation requires a delicate balance. Don't ignore their need for attention, but don't give them more than they deserve either. Praise their accomplishments, but do so in a way that feels authentic. If they're expecting praise for something that's not all that impressive, give it to them in a measured way. Praise their effort, but don't go overboard. You want them to feel recognized, but you don't want them to think their every move is deserving of a standing ovation. It's a fine line, but with practice, you'll learn how to navigate it without getting caught up in the drama.

Lastly, you'll need to set boundaries. The Diva's tendency to dominate conversations and take over projects can be exhausting. Be clear about when they've crossed a line, especially if their antics are affecting the team or the work. If they insist on making every project about them, gently remind them of the collective effort. Encourage collaboration and steer the focus back to the team's success, not just their own. It's not about deflating their ego, but about ensuring the work gets done without their drama derailing progress.

In the end, managing the Diva is about finding a balance between acknowledging their strengths and mitigating their weaknesses. Keep your cool, stay professional, and don't let them drag you into their dramatic whirlwind. With the right approach, you can work with the Diva without losing your mind—though you may need a bit of patience and a strong sense of humor to survive the ride.

Self-Assessment – Which Type is Your Boss?

To truly understand how to tame your boss, you first need to identify which type you're dealing with. The following self-assessment will help you pinpoint your boss's behavior and give you the clarity you need to navigate their quirks. For each set of questions, rate your boss's behavior using the following 1–5 scale:

1 – Not at all
2 – Rarely
3 – Sometimes
4 – Often
5 – Always

Answer honestly. The more accurate your assessment, the more effective your strategies for managing them will be.

The Control Freak

1. To what extent does your boss insist on overseeing every detail of your work, even when it's unnecessary?
2. To what extent does your boss micromanage meetings, ensuring that every action item is followed up on precisely as planned?
3. To what extent does your boss seem uncomfortable or anxious when things don't go according to their vision, requiring immediate correction?

The Ghost Boss

1. To what extent does your boss avoid face-to-face interaction, even when it's crucial for project success?
2. To what extent does your boss seem unavailable or unresponsive when you need guidance or approval?
3. To what extent does your boss leave important decisions to others, only to swoop in when the outcome is either a success or failure?

The Cheerleader

1. To what extent does your boss frequently shower you and the team with praise, even when it feels undeserved?
2. To what extent does your boss emphasize positivity, often glossing over problems or challenges that require attention?
3. To what extent does your boss encourage you to be "better" or "more positive," even when circumstances suggest a more realistic approach?

The Volcano

1. To what extent does your boss have outbursts of anger or frustration that seem disproportionate to the issue at hand?
2. To what extent does your boss create tension in the workplace by reacting unpredictably or erupting during stressful

situations?

3. To what extent does your boss make you feel like you're walking on eggshells, unsure of when the next emotional outburst might happen?

The Visionary

1. To what extent does your boss propose ambitious, big-picture ideas that are not always practical or achievable?
2. To what extent does your boss seem more focused on future possibilities than on the present realities or day-to-day operations?
3. To what extent does your boss expect you to share their vision, even when the details or execution aren't clear?

The Spreadsheet Overlord

1. To what extent does your boss use data, spreadsheets, and numbers to make decisions, often disregarding intuition or gut feeling?
2. To what extent does your boss want every project to be meticulously tracked, monitored, and reported, even for minor tasks?
3. To what extent does your boss rely on complex formulas and metrics to evaluate success, sometimes making simple solutions feel overly complicated?

The Social Butterfly

1. To what extent does your boss prioritize attending social events, networking, and office gossip over actual work?
2. To what extent does your boss value relationships and social dynamics in the office more than results or productivity?
3. To what extent does your boss appear to focus on making personal connections rather than pushing forward on critical business matters?

The Rulebook

1. To what extent does your boss stick rigidly to company policies and procedures, even when flexibility might benefit the situation?
2. To what extent does your boss seem uncomfortable with any suggestion that deviates from established rules or practices?
3. To what extent does your boss rely on formal protocols, even when they seem unnecessary or outdated?

The Idea Tornado

1. To what extent does your boss frequently propose new ideas or projects, often abandoning them before they've been fully implemented?
2. To what extent does your boss encourage brainstorming and

creativity, but rarely follows through on ideas once they're introduced?
3. To what extent does your boss struggle to prioritize or focus on one project at a time, constantly bouncing between new ideas?

The Zen Master

1. To what extent does your boss remain calm and unflappable, even during stressful or chaotic situations?
2. To what extent does your boss seem detached from the day-to-day operations or emotionally disengaged from the team's struggles?
3. To what extent does your boss offer advice that's overly simplistic or philosophical, even when practical solutions are needed?

The Insomniac

1. To what extent does your boss send emails or messages during late hours, expecting immediate responses at all times?
2. To what extent does your boss appear to work tirelessly, often staying late and demanding others to match their level of commitment?
3. To what extent does your boss expect you to always be available, no matter the time of day or your own workload?

T he Diva

1. To what extent does your boss demand constant attention, praise, and recognition from you and the team?
2. To what extent does your boss create drama or make minor issues seem like major crises to grab the spotlight?
3. To what extent does your boss rely on their charisma or image, expecting others to cater to their needs and desires?

N ow, Calculate Your Results
Once you've answered the questions, tally up your scores for each boss type. The higher your score in a given category, the more likely that your boss exhibits that particular type of behavior.

- A total score of 10-15 for any type indicates that your boss likely exhibits traits of that type.
- A score of 1-9 suggests that this behavior isn't a major part of their leadership style.
- If you find yourself scoring equally high across multiple types, congratulations, you've got yourself a complicated boss who may embody several of these behaviors. Don't worry; you'll still be able to use this book to survive the madness.

Now that you've pinpointed your boss's type, it's time to use the strategies in this book to manage the relationship, maintain your sanity, and maybe even come out of it unscathed.

Conclusion: Taming the Beast, One Boss at a Time

So, you've made it this far. You've learned about the 12 distinct boss types, from the micromanaging Control Freak to the ever-elusive Ghost Boss, and you've taken the time to figure out which one (or more) you're dealing with. Congratulations. You're now armed with the knowledge to survive and, dare I say, thrive in your workplace without losing your mind.

Let's take a moment to review these boss archetypes. First, there's *The Control Freak*, who will likely follow up on your email every hour just to make sure you're getting the tiniest detail right. They have a crippling need for certainty and a distrust of anything they can't directly monitor. Then we have *The Ghost Boss*, who is there in body but invisible when you need them. Emails remain unanswered, and decisions are left to linger while they're off doing whatever mysterious thing it is that makes them disappear. A close cousin to the Ghost Boss is *The Cheerleader*—positive, optimistic, sometimes ridiculously so, but blissfully unaware of the pile of issues accumulating around them while they're busy high-fiving everyone.

Then there's *The Volcano*, a walking time bomb of explosive emotions. One minute you're basking in the glow of a productive conversation, and the next, you're wondering if you've somehow offended them, as the lava begins to flow. The *Visionary* is next in line—big dreams, lofty ideas, and very little sense of the practicality required to make them happen. They inspire you to look beyond the horizon while leaving you questioning whether anyone's actually supposed to steer the ship.

At the other end of the spectrum, we have the *Spreadsheet Overlord*, the lover of data, numbers, and charts. Every decision is made based on stats and figures, and the poor soul who dares to suggest a decision driven by experience or intuition may be met with a cold, calculating stare. Then there's *The Social Butterfly*, fluttering from conversation to conversation, more concerned with networking than actually getting anything done. *The Rulebook* comes right after, forever clutching policies and procedures, turning every task into a bureaucratic maze that only the most determined will navigate successfully.

The Idea Tornado is a whirlwind of new concepts, a veritable fountain of creativity that never quite lands on anything concrete. While you're still recovering from one idea, they've already moved on to the next. The *Zen Master*—calm, serene, and entirely disconnected from reality—brings balance to chaos, but perhaps too much. If only they could offer more direction when things are on fire.

Next, we have *The Insomniac*, a workaholic who expects the same tireless commitment from everyone else. The late-night emails, the unreasonably tight deadlines—they never seem to turn off, and they expect you to follow suit. And last, but certainly not least, there's *The Diva*. This is the boss who thrives on drama, attention, and power. It's all about them—always. Everyone else exists to serve their need for validation and constant adoration.

Now, how do you actually deal with all of this? It's simple, really. You've got to work with what you've got. If you've got a *Control Freak*, learn to provide regular updates to keep them at bay. For the *Ghost Boss*, you may need to take more initiative and be prepared to fill in the gaps when they're absent. *The Cheerleader*? Let their optimism fuel your own, but don't forget the realities lurking beneath. With *The Volcano*, brace yourself for occasional eruptions, but be quick to manage the fallout—don't get sucked into their drama.

As for *The Visionary*, keep their ideas alive by helping translate them into actionable steps. With the *Spreadsheet Overlord*, show that you can play the data game too, but also don't be afraid to ask for a little human insight. *The Social Butterfly* will need to be gently redirected towards results when it's time to work. For *The Rulebook*, respect the system, but don't be afraid to suggest a bit of flexibility when needed. *The Idea Tornado* requires grounding—help them focus, take one project at a time, and prioritize.

The *Zen Master* needs reminders of the day-to-day pressures of the business, as their calm detachment can often feel out of touch. For the *Insomniac*, manage your boundaries—learn how to say no, and don't be afraid to push back on unrealistic expectations. Finally, with the *Diva*, establish firm boundaries early and manage their attention-seeking behaviors with diplomacy. Don't fall for the drama.

In the end, no boss is perfect. They're all a mix of strengths, weaknesses, and quirks, just like the rest of us. But armed with a solid understanding of what makes your boss tick, you can better navigate their behaviors, manage your own reactions, and come out on top. After all, your success doesn't just rely on your own hard work—it's about mastering the art of working with people, including your boss. With the right strategies, you can not only survive under any of these 12 types but thrive despite them. Now, go ahead, take charge, and show your boss just how it's done.

The End

About the Author

Marako Marcus is a consultant, coach, and public speaker with a reputation for being straight to the point—no fluff, no excuses. He helps executives, teams, and individuals face their challenges head-on, cutting through the corporate nonsense and delivering results that matter. With years of experience working with organizations of all sizes, Marako knows exactly what's wrong with most workplaces and how to fix them—without the usual corporate jargon.

A master of tough love and tough conversations, he's a coach who tells it like it is and makes sure you know exactly where you stand. His approach is simple: if you're not getting it done, stop whining and start acting. He's worked with leaders who need a wake-up call and teams who need someone to light a fire under them.

When he's not stirring up success in the business world, Marako unleashes his creativity as a musician. Yes, he's the guy who can juggle spreadsheets and compose a killer track at the same time—proving that sharp focus can strike the right chord in both the boardroom and the studio. Marako's blend of directness and creativity makes him a unique voice in the business world—and someone you'll want to listen to.

Book Links available at https://linktr.ee/marakomarcusbooks

www.ingramcontent.com/pod-product-compliance
Lightning Source LLC
Chambersburg PA
CBHW071111240526
45469CB00006BD/2430